W9-CLF-496

Tools We Use
Doctors

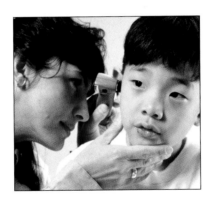

Dana Meachen Rau

Marshall Cavendish
Benchmark
New York

Feeling bad?

You may need to go to
the doctor.

A doctor's waiting room
has toys.

Children can play while
they wait.

Doctors wear white coats.

They keep a big folder all about you.

The doctor weighs you on a scale.

She measures you with a tall ruler.

You sit on a doctor's table.

She is ready to give you your checkup.

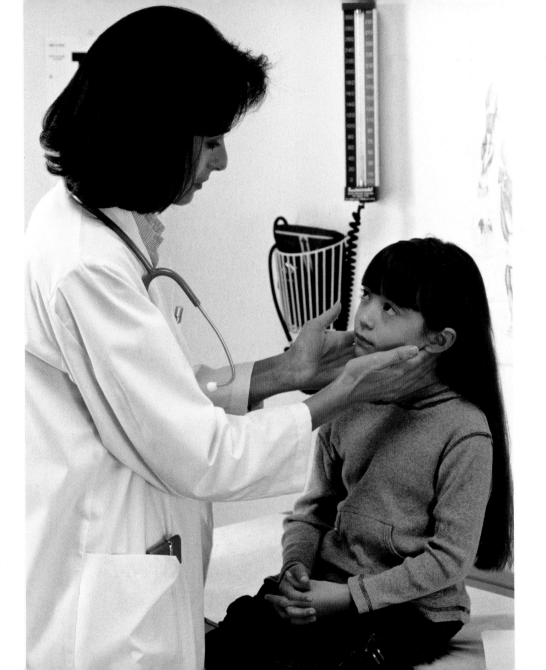

She listens to your heart
with a *stethoscope*.

She can hear you breathe
with it, too.

She takes your *temperature*.

She looks in your eyes and ears.

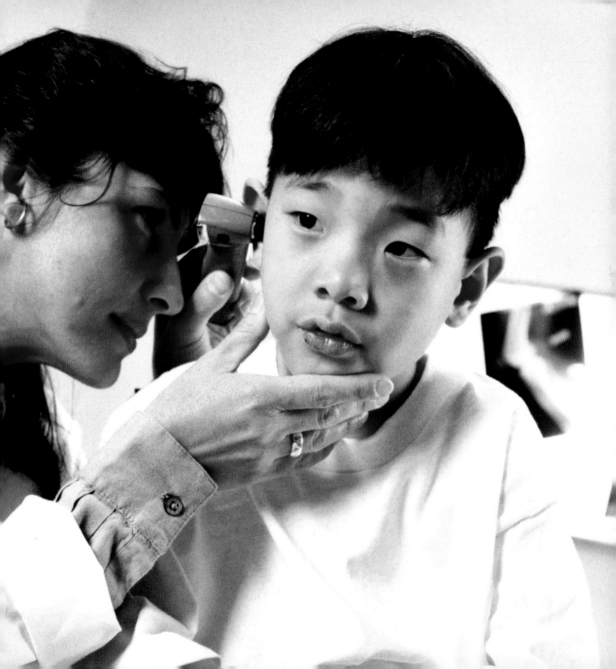

Some children may need medicine.

Medicine can be pills or a drink.

Medicine is sometimes a shot.

Then the doctor puts a bandage on you.

A big cut might need *stitches*.

Stitches help close the cut.

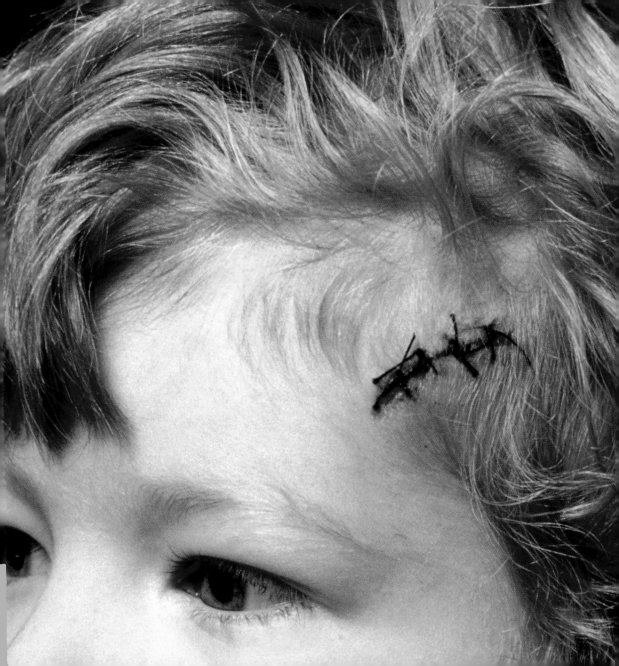

An X-ray is a picture of your bones.

The doctor can see if a bone is broken.

A cast helps a broken bone *heal*.

The cast holds your bone straight.

Doctors use their tools to check your body.

They help you feel well again.

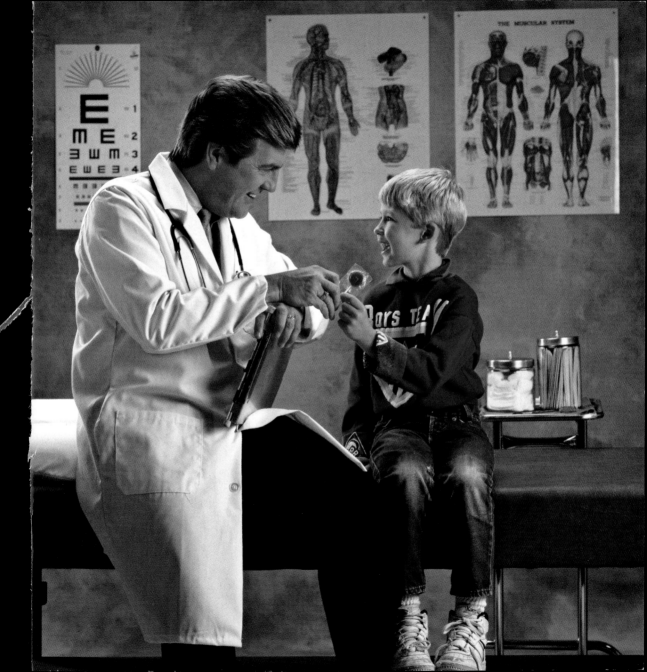

Tools Doctors Use

bandage

cast

medicine

stethoscope

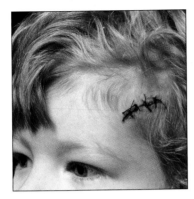

stitches

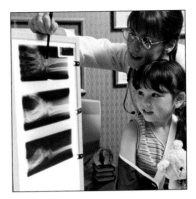

X-ray

Challenge Words

heal (HEEL) To get better.

stethoscope (STETH-uh-skohp) A tool doctors use to listen to your heart and lungs.

stitches (STICH-es) Bits of thread used to sew the sides of a cut together.

temperature (TEM-pruh-chuhr) How hot or cold your body is.

29

Index

Page numbers in **boldface** are illustrations.

bandage, 18, **19**, **28**
body, 26
bones, 22, **23**, 24
breathe, 12
broken bone, 22, 24

cast, 24, **25**, **28**
checkup, 10
cuts, 20, **21**

doctor, 2, 4, 6, **7**, 8, 10, 26

ears, 14, **15**
eyes, 14

folder, 6, **7**

heal, 24, 29
heart, 12

measure, 8, **9**
medicine, 16, **17**, 18, **28**

pills, 16

ruler, 8

scale, 8
shot, 18, **19**
stethoscope, 12, **13**, **28**, 29
stitches, 20, **21**, **29**

table, 10, **11**
temperature, 14, 29
toys, 4, **5**

waiting room, 4, **5**
weigh, 8
well, 26
white coat, 6, **7**

X-ray, 22, **23**, **29**

About the Author

Dana Meachen Rau is an author, editor, and illustrator. A graduate of Trinity College in Hartford, Connecticut, she has written more than one hundred fifty books for children, including nonfiction, biographies, early readers, and historical fiction. She lives with her family in Burlington, Connecticut.

With thanks to the Reading Consultants:

Nanci Vargus, Ed.D., is an Assistant Professor of Elementary Education at the University of Indianapolis.

Beth Walker Gambro received her M.S. Ed. Reading from the University of St. Francis, Joliet, Illinois.

Marshall Cavendish Benchmark
99 White Plains Road
Tarrytown, New York 10591-9001
www.marshallcavendish.us

Library of Congress Cataloging-in-Publication Data

Rau, Dana Meachen, 1971–
Doctors / by Dana Meachen Rau.
p. cm. — (Bookworms. Tools we use)
Summary: "Introduces tools doctors use in their work"—Provided by publisher.
Includes index.
ISBN 978-0-7614-2659-2
1. Physicians—Juvenile literature. I. Title. II. Series.
R707.R3844 2007
610.92—dc22
2006035145

Editor: Christina Gardeski
Publisher: Michelle Bisson
Designer: Virginia Pope
Art Director: Anahid Hamparian

Photo Research by Anne Burns Images

Cover Photo by *Corbis*/Mark Adams

The photographs in this book are used with permission and through the courtesy of:
SuperStock: pp. 1, 15 age fotostock. *Photo Researchers*: p. 3 Ken Cavanagh;
pp. 21, 29L Chris Priest. *Corbis*: p. 5 Jose Luis Pelaez, Inc.; p. 9 Michael Keller;
p. 11 LWA Stephen Welstead; pp. 13, 28BR Royalty Free; pp. 17, 28BL Ed Bock;
pp. 23, 29 R Roy Morsch; pp. 25, 28TR Warren Morgan; p. 27 Steve Chenn.
Custom Medical Stock Photos: p. 7. *Getty Images*: pp. 19, 28TL.

Printed in Malaysia
1   3   5   6   4   2